Fairs Then and Now

Christine Butterworth

Nelson

Contents

Fairs	4
Nottingham Goose Fair	5
Fairs in London	6
What People saw at the Fair	8
What People did at the Fair	13
Rides at the Fair	14
Index	16

Fairs

There have been fairs for a very long time. It is always fun to go to a fair. People love to go on the rides.

Nottingham Goose Fair

The first fairs were markets.

Nottingham had its first fair a thousand years ago. People came to buy and sell geese.

Nottingham still has a Goose Fair held every year, but there are no geese now!

It is a big funfair.

Fairs in London

The city of London had lots of fairs. By the 16th century, when Queen Elizabeth the First was on the throne, fairs were more than just markets. People came to have fun.

An Elizabethan fair

The May Fair was held in London in the 18th century. Mayfair in London is named after this fair.

The May Fair in London in 18th century

What People saw at the Fair

People came to see strange and wonderful things.

They saw some very strange animals.

a sheep with two heads

dancing dogs

At a London fair in 1660, people came to see a famous strong man.

He could lift part of a heavy cannon with his hair.

In 1667, people saw a very small girl.
She was sixteen years old, but she was only 45 centimetres tall.
A man who saw her said, 'She reads very well, sings and whistles.'

What People did at the Fair

Everyone liked to eat and drink at the fair. They still do!

People came to the fair to get toys and dolls. They still do!

Rides at the fair

Fairs had swings for hundreds of years.

A Victorian swing

Then a hundred years ago, the first rides with motors were made.
Now, rides with motors can go fast.

A swing ride now

Today the rides are faster than ever.
The fair at Blackpool has a roller-coaster called
'The Big One'.
It goes at 120 kmph and is over 60 m tall.
It is one of the biggest and fastest roller-coasters
in the world.

'The Big One' at Blackpool

Index

Acrobats 8

Blackpool 15

Dodgems 4

Food and drink 12

Ghost train 4

Goose Fair 5

Jugglers 8

May Fair 7

Queen Elizabeth the First 6

Roller-coaster 15

Roundabout 4

Small girl 11

Strong man 10

Swings 4, 14

Toys 13